This Book Belongs To

_____

For A Special Friend

Ariel Books

Andrews and McMeel
Kansas City

10 9 8

ISBN: 0-8362-3000-0

Library of Congress Catalog Card Number:
91-77107

BOOK DESIGN BY JUDITH A. STAGNITTO

Close friends are truly life's treasures. Sometimes they know us better than we know ourselves. With gentle honesty, they are there to guide us and support us, to share our laughter and our tears. Their presence reminds us that no matter what, we're not alone.

This little book, filled with warmth and gratitude, is a happy celebration of friendship and its place in our lives. A joy shared is twice a joy, a sorrow shared is half a sorrow. And a friendship found is a blessing that multiplies daily.

For A
Special
Friend

Like everyone else I feel the need of relations and friendship, of affection, of friendly intercourse, and I am not made of stone or iron, so I cannot miss these things without feeling, as does any other intelligent man, a void and deep need. I tell you this to let you know how much good your visit has done me.

—*Vincent van Gogh*

It is not so much our friends'
help that helps us as the confi-
dent knowledge that they will
help us.

—*Epicurus*

Life without a friend is like death
without a witness.

—*Spanish Proverb*

The best way to keep your
friends is not to give them away.

—*Wilson Mizner*

The happiest moments my heart
knows are those in which it is
pouring forth its affections to a
few esteemed characters.

—*Thomas Jefferson*

One can never speak enough of
the virtues, the dangers, the
power of shared laughter.

—Francoise Sagan

Friendship is always a sweet
responsibility, never an
opportunity.

—Kahlil Gibran

There is a magic in the memory of schoolboy friendships; it softens the heart, and even affects the nervous system of those who have no heart.

—*Benjamin Disraeli*

I no doubt deserved my enemies, but I don't believe I deserved my friends.

—*Walt Whitman*

True friendship is never serene,

—*Marquise de Sévigné*

When friends stop being frank
and useful to each other, the
whole world loses some of its
radiance.

—*Anatole Broyard*

Friends are born, not made.

—*Henry Adams*

Friendship is a single soul dwelling in two bodies.

—*Aristotle*

A new friend is like new wine; when it has aged you will drink it with pleasure.

—*Ecclesiastes* 9:10

It is one of the blessings of old friends that you can afford to be stupid with them.

—*Ralph Waldo Emerson*

One loyal friend is worth ten thousand relatives.

—*Euripides*

This communicating of a man's self to his friend works two contrary effects; for it redoubleth joys, and cutteth griefs in half.

—*Francis Bacon*

Your friend is the man who knows all about you, and still likes you.

—*Elbert Hubbard*

A friend should be a master at
guessing and keeping still.

—*Friedrich Nietzsche*

Life is partly what we make it,
and partly what it is made by the
friends whom we choose.

—*Tehyi Hsieh*

The only thing to do is to hug one's friends tight and do one's job.

—*Edith Wharton*

A friend may well be reckoned the masterpiece of nature.

—*Ralph Waldo Emerson*

There is no hope of joy except in human relations.

—*Antoine de Sainte-Exupéry*

The making of friends, who are real friends, is the best token we have of a man's success in life.

—*Edward Everett Hale*

The proper office of a friend is to side with you when you are in the wrong. Nearly anybody will side with you when you are in the right.

—*Mark Twain*

Except in cases of necessity,
which are rare, leave your friend
to learn unpleasant things from
his enemies; they are ready
enough to tell them.

—*Oliver Wendell Holmes*

Little do men perceive what solitude is, and how far it extendeth. For a crowd is not company, and faces are but a gallery of pictures, and talk but a tinkling cymbal, where there is no love.

—*Francis Bacon*

The most I can do for my friend is simply to be his friend. I have no wealth to bestow on him. If he knows that I am happy in loving him, he will want no other reward. Is not friendship divine in this?

—Henry David Thoreau

Friendship that flows from the heart cannot be frozen by adversity, as the water that flows from the spring cannot congeal in winter.

—*James Fenimore Cooper*

Those that want friends to open
themselves unto are cannibals of
their own hearts.

—*Francis Bacon*

A friend to all is a friend to none.

—*Aristotle*

Friendship without self-interest is
one of the rare and beautiful
things in life.

—*James Francis Byrnes*

Friendship is the only thing in the
world concerning the usefulness
of which all mankind are agreed.

—*Cicero*

I do not wish to treat friendships daintily, but with roughest courage. When they are real, they are not glass threads or frost-work, but the solidest thing we know.

—*Ralph Waldo Emerson*

Do not save your loving speeches
For your friends till they are
    dead;
Do not write them on their
    tombstones,
Speak them rather now instead.

—*Anna Cummins*

True friendship's laws are by this
   rule express'd,
Welcome the coming, speed the
   parting guest.

           —Alexander Pope

Every man should have a fair-
sized cemetery in which to bury
the faults of his friends.

           —Henry Brooks Adams

No distance of place or lapse of time can lessen the friendship of those who are thoroughly persuaded of each other's worth.

—*Robert Southey*

If a man does not make new acquaintances as he advances through life, he will soon find himself alone. A man, sir, should keep his friendships in constant repair.

—*Dr. Johnson*

Those friends thou hast and
their adoption tried,
Grapple them to thy soul with
hoops of steel;
But do not dull thy palm with
entertainment
Of each new-hatch'd, unfledg'd
comrade.

—*William Shakespeare*

Friendship is a thing most necessary to life, since without friends no one would choose to live, though possessed of all other advantages.

—*Aristotle*

The feeling of friendship is like that of being comfortably filled with roast beef; love, like being enlivened with champagne.

—*Dr. Johnson*

When true friends meet in
   adverse hour,
'Tis like a sunbeam through a
   shower.
A watery way an instant seen,
The darkly closing clouds
   between.

—*Sir Walter Scott*

When my friends are one-eyed, I look at their profile.

—*Joseph Joubert*

A friend is a present you give yourself.

—*Robert Louis Stevenson*

Nothing makes the earth seem so spacious as to have friends at a distance; they make the latitudes and the longitudes.

—*Henry David Thoreau*

If we would build on a sure foundation in friendship, we must love our friends for their sakes rather than for our own.

—*Charlotte Brontë*

It is a wonderful advantage to a man, in every pursuit or avocation, to secure an adviser in a sensible woman. In woman there is at once a subtle delicacy of tact, and a plain soundness of judgment, which are rarely combined to an equal degree in man. A woman, if she be really your friend, will have a sensitive regard for your character, honor, repute. She will seldom counsel you to

do a shabby thing; for a woman
friend always desires to be proud
of you.

—*Sir Edward Bulwer-Lytton*

Friendship is not possible
between two women one of
whom is very well dressed.

—*Laurie Colwin*

Be in peace with many, but let
one of a thousand be thy
counsellor.

—*Ecclesiastes* 1:23

Anybody can sympathize with the suffering of a friend, but it requires a very fine nature to sympathize with a friend's success.

—*Oscar Wilde*

Better be a nettle in the side of your friend than his echo.

—*Ralph Waldo Emerson*

I have lost friends, some by death...others by sheer inability to cross the street.

—*Virginia Woolf*

My coat and I live comfortably together. It has assumed all my wrinkles, does not hurt me anywhere, has moulded itself on my deformities, and is complacent to all my movements, and I only feel its presence because it keeps me warm. Old coats and old friends are the same thing.

—*Victor Hugo*

If I mayn't tell you what I feel,
what is the use of a friend?

—*William Makepeace Thackeray*

It is the friends you can call up at
4 A.M. that matter.

—*Marlene Dietrich*

Not chance of birth or place has
    made us friends,
Being oftentimes of different
    tongues and nations,
But the endeavor for the selfsame
    ends,
With the same hopes, and fears,
    and aspirations.

—*Henry Wadsworth Longfellow*

A man cannot speak to his son, but as a father; to his wife, but as a husband; to his enemy, but upon terms: whereas a friend may speak, as the case requires, and not as it sorteth with the person.

—*Francis Bacon*

It is only the great-hearted who can be true friends. The mean and cowardly can never know what true friendship means.

—*Charles Kingsley*

I was the kid next door's imaginary friend.

—Emo Phillips

The lion and the calf shall lie down together, but the calf won't get much sleep.

—Woody Allen

A friendship will be young after
the lapse of half a century; a pas-
sion is old at the end of three
months.

—*Madame Swetchine*

Friendship based solely upon
gratitude is like a photograph;
with time it fades.

—*Carmen Sylva*

If a friend of mine gave a feast, and did not invite me to it, I should not mind a bit. But if a friend of mine had a sorrow and refused to allow me to share it, I should feel it most bitterly. If he shut the doors of the house of mourning against me, I would move back again and again and beg to be admitted so that I might share in what I was entitled to share. If he thought me

unworthy, unfit to weep with
him, I should feel it as the most
poignant humiliation.

—*Oscar Wilde*

I breathed a song into the air,
It fell to earth, I knew not where;
For who has sight so keen and
strong,
That it can follow the flight of
song—

The song from beginning to end,
I found again in the heart of a
friend.

—*Henry Wadsworth Longfellow*

So long as we are loved by others,
I would almost say that we are
indispensable; and no man is
useless while he has a friend.

    —*Robert Louis Stevenson*

No man is the whole of himself.
His friends are the rest of him.
—*Good Life Almanac*

The best mirror is an old friend.

—*Proverb*

It is the first law of friendship that it has to be cultivated. The second is to be indulgent when the first law is neglected.

—*Voltaire*

People will, in a great degree, and not without reason, form their opinion of you upon that which they have of your friends; and there is a Spanish proverb which says very justly, "Tell me whom you live with, and I will tell you who you are."

—Lord Chesterfield

Fame is the scentless sunflower,
with gaudy crown of gold;
But friendship is the breathing
rose, with sweets in every fold.
—*Oliver Wendell Holmes*

I have lost my seven best friends,
which is to say that God has had
mercy on me seven times without
realizing it. He lent a friendship,
took it from me, and sent me
another.

—*Jean Cocteau*

The difference between men friends and women friends is that men tend to do things together, women tend to just be together.

—*Art Jahnke*

My father and he had one of those English friendships which begins by avoiding intimacies and eventually eliminates speech altogether.

—*Jorge Luis Borges*

My God, this is a hell of a job. I have no trouble with my enemies. I can take care of my enemies all right. But my damn friends, my goddamn friends. They're the ones that keep me walking the floor at night.

—*Warren G. Harding*

Money can't buy friends but it can get you a better class of enemy.

—*Spike Milligan*

However rare true love may be, it is less so than true friendship.

—*François, Duc de La Rochefoucauld*

The easiest kind of relationship for me is with ten thousand people. The hardest is with one.

—*Joan Baez*

Chance makes our parents, but choice makes our friends.

—*Jacques Delille*

Real friendships among men are so rare that when they occur they are famous.

—*Clarence Day*

We make our friends; we make
our enemies; but God makes our
next-door neighbour.

—*G. K. Chesterton*

Friends are God's apology for relations.

—*Hugh Kingsmill*

Love demands infinitely less than friendship.

—*George Jean Nathan*

A benevolent man should allow a few faults in himself, to keep his friends in countenance.

—*Benjamin Franklin*

A friendship that can end never really began.

—*Publilius Syrus*

Talk not of wasted affection,
affection never was wasted.
   —Henry Wadsworth Longfellow

A friend is one before whom I
can think aloud.

   —Ralph Waldo Emerson

We can never replace a friend. When a man is fortunate enough to have several, he finds they are all different. No one has a double in friendship.

—*Johann Schiller*

Choose a friend as thou dost a wife, till death separate you.

—*William Penn*

The supreme happiness of life is the conviction of being loved for yourself, or, more correctly, being loved in spite of yourself.

—*Victor Hugo*